Lives and Times

NELSON MANDELA

Jayne Woodhouse

Heinemann
LIBRARY

www.heinemann.co.uk

Visit our website to find out more information about Heinemann Library books.

To order:

 Phone 44 (0) 1865 888066

 Send a fax to 44 (0) 1865 314091

Visit the Heinemann Bookshop at www.heinemann.co.uk to browse our catalogue and order online.

First published in Great Britain by Heinemann Library,
Halley Court, Jordan Hill, Oxford OX2 8EJ,
a division of Reed Educational and Professional Publishing Ltd.
Heinemann is a registered trademark of Reed Educational and Professional Publishing Ltd.

OXFORD MELBOURNE AUCKLAND
JOHANNESBURG BLANTYRE GABORONE
IBADAN PORTSMOUTH (NH) USA CHICAGO

Designed by Ken Vail Graphic Design, Cambridge
Illustrated by Sean Victory
Originated by Dot Gradations
Printed by South China Printing in Hong Kong/China

ISBN 0 431 13443 X (hardback)   ISBN 0 431 13448 0 (paperback)
05 04 03 02 01   05 04 03 02 01
10 9 8 7 6 5 4 3 2 1   10 9 8 7 6 5 4 3 2 1

British Library Cataloguing in Publication Data

Woodhouse, Jayne
    Nelson Mandela. – (Lives and times) (Take-off!)
    1.Mandela, Nelson, 1918– – Juvenile literature
    2.Presidents – South Africa – Biography – Juvenile literature
    3.Anti-apartheid movements – South Africa – History – Juvenile literature
    I.Title
    968'.06'092

Acknowledgements

The publishers would like to thank the following for permission to reproduce photographs: The British Library Newspaper Library, with permission from The Daily Mirror, The Independent, The Pretoria News and The Star: pp21–22; Britstock – IFA: Haga p23; Chris Honeywell: p18; Link Picture Library: G English p17; Magnum Photos Ltd: I Berry p16, G Mendal p19; Rex Features: N Berman p22

Cover photograph reproduced with permission of Universal Pictorial Press.

Our thanks to Sue Graves and Hilda Reed for their advice and expertise in the preparation of this book.

Every effort has been made to contact copyright holders of any material reproduced in this book. Any omissions will be rectified in subsequent printings if notice is given to the publishers.

Contents

Any words appearing in the text in bold, **like this**, are explained in the Glossary.

Childhood

This book is about a very important person. His name is Nelson Mandela. He was born in 1918 in South Africa.

Nelson was born near Umtata.

A map of South Africa.

UNITED KINGDOM

AFRICA

SOUTH AFRICA

JOHANNESBURG

UMTATA

CAPE TOWN

mud house

grass roof

The small village where Nelson grew up.

Nelson was the son of a **Thembu** chief. His African name is Rolihlala, which means 'troublemaker'! Nelson grew up in a small village. His home was made of mud. It had a grass roof.

Growing up

When Nelson was five years old, he began to look after the family's sheep and **calves**. He loved to play with the other boys in the **veld**.

Nelson looking after the family's sheep.

Later, Nelson went to school and then to **university**. He became a **lawyer** in **Johannesburg**.

Nelson Mandela working as a lawyer.

Kept apart

Both black and white people live in South Africa. At that time white people ruled the country and made **laws**. They kept the best houses, schools and land for themselves.

White people living in a nice, big house.

Black people living in a poor area.

They said that all black people must live apart from white people. The South African word for this law is **apartheid**. It made life very hard for black people.

Prison

Mandela and his friends knew that **apartheid** was wrong. They knew that they had to work hard to change the **laws**.

Mandela

Mandela and his friends talking about getting the laws changed.

Mandela was kept in prison for 27 years.

The white people who ruled South Africa did not want to change the laws. In 1963, they arrested Mandela and sent him to prison.

Mandela in prison.

Free at last

People all over the world thought that Mandela was right. They wanted life in South Africa to change. People shouted, 'Free Nelson Mandela!' at **demonstrations**.

People at a demonstration to set Mandela free.

Nelson Mandela

Nelson's wife Winnie

Mandela on his first day of freedom.

At last, in 1990, Mandela was set free. He was 71 years old.

President

Four years later, in 1994, there was an **election** in South Africa. For the first time, black people as well as white people were allowed to **vote**.

voters

Black and white people waiting to vote.

Nelson Mandela as the president of South Africa.

They chose Nelson Mandela to be the
president of South Africa. The man who was
a prisoner for so long had helped to change
the lives of his people.

Photographs

Photographs show us what Nelson Mandela looks like. This picture was taken when he was a young man.

This is Nelson Mandela as a young man.

Compare this photograph of Mandela with the one on page 17. In what ways does he look different now?

Nelson Mandela

Nelson's wife
Winnie

This photograph was taken when
Mandela was released from prison.

Many photographs were taken of Mandela
when he was set free from prison. Millions of
people all around the world watched this on
television, as it was happening.

Books

Mandela has written a book telling the story of his life. It is called *Long Walk to Freedom*. It tells us about his feelings and friends and what it was like in prison.

Nelson Mandela's book about his life.

When someone writes a book about his or her life, it is called an autobiography.

Posters

posters

Posters made when Mandela was still in prison.

We still have posters from the time when Mandela was in prison. They say that he should be set free.

Newspapers

We can read all about Mandela's life in the newspapers. They wrote about him in different ways at different times. Can you see how?

TWO BIG ROYAL VISITS OF THE YEAR

DAILY MIRROR, Wednesday, July 10, 1996 Page 9

12,000 EYES ON NELSON

Now Big Daddy worked miracle

By MERVYN REES in Cape Town

MAKING WAVES: Mandela rides with the Queen. Pictures: KENT GAVIN and ALISDAIR MACDONALD

EYE-EYE: One guardsman sneaks a look

LEADER : Prince Philip follows Mandela

Queen greets hero Mandela

By JAMES WHITAKER

ALL eyes were on Nelson Mandela yesterday when the People's Hero took London by storm.

Mandela in London: South Africans who fled from apartheid into exile can feel proud of their nation – and cry a

Grand tour: The Queen and Nelson Mandela enjoying the acclaim of the crowds outside Buckingham Palace

Photograph: Glynn Griffiths

The man who made a rainbow shine

RAYMOND WHITAKER

more," said a veteran of such   Africa in the apartheid years   in South Africa, and that peo-   Under   apartheid   Mr   railing on the Mall to ensure   a Swazi prince, but the presi-

All around us

Some places have statues of Nelson Mandela. Streets and buildings have been named after him, too.

A man making a statue of Nelson Mandela.

statue

Look out for any streets or buildings named after Nelson Mandela.

People wanting to see Mandela when he came to London in 1996.

You may know someone who has been on holiday to South Africa. You may even know someone who has lived there. They may be able to tell you more about Nelson Mandela.

Glossary

apartheid when black people and white people are kept apart. You say *a-par-tide*.

calves young cows. You say *carves*.

demonstrate get together with others as a way of showing your beliefs

election when people get a chance to choose who will govern their country

Johannesburg a very large and important city in South Africa. You say *jo-han-es-berg*.

laws the rules of a country

lawyer someone who studies the rules of a country

president the leader of a country

Thembu an African tribe or group who have lived in South Africa for hundreds of years. You say *tem-boo*.

university a place to go on to for more study, after you have finished school

veld a South African word meaning open countryside. You say *velt*.

vote choosing who you want to be in the government

Index

24

Titles in the *Lives and Times* series include:

Hardback   0 431 13440 5

Hardback   0 431 13442 1

Hardback   0 431 13443 X

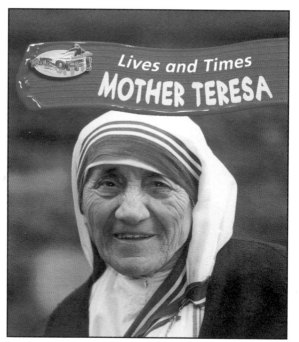

Hardback   0 431 13441 3

Find out about the other titles in this series on our website www.heinemann.co.uk/library